What Do We Know About
Bigfoot?

by Steve Korté

illustrated by Manuel Gutierrez

Penguin Workshop

For Juliette—SK

For Colibrí—MG

PENGUIN WORKSHOP
An imprint of Penguin Random House LLC, New York

First published in the United States of America by Penguin Workshop,
an imprint of Penguin Random House LLC, New York, 2022

Visit us online at penguinrandomhouse.com.

Library of Congress Cataloging-in-Publication Data is available.

Printed in the United States of America

ISBN 9780593386699 (paperback)   10 9 8
ISBN 9780593386705 (library binding)   10 9 8 7 6 5 4 3 2

Contents

What Do We Know About Bigfoot?

In the summer of 2012, a woman was walking down a long, deserted road in the Hoopa Valley Tribal reservation in Northern California. It was nighttime, and she carried a flashlight so she could find her way along the dark road. Her name was Sadie McCovey, and she was about to have a disturbing experience that she would remember for the rest of her life.

An eerie suspicion overcame Sadie. She felt as if something was behind her, watching her. She was afraid it wanted to overtake her, or even to capture her. She became very scared.

Sadie turned around and pointed her flashlight behind her. Not far from her was something that appeared to be a giant human or an apelike creature she had never seen before. It was crouching low to

the ground on its two legs. Its eyes glowed green in the glare of her flashlight. Sadie screamed.

"You could see the hair spiking around its face and the body," Sadie remembered. "As I screamed, it got up and turned around and just walked off."

Sadie shivered for a moment at the memory of this encounter, and then she added, "I knew for sure it was Bigfoot."

In North America, there have been many sightings of a large, powerful beast that has come to be known as Bigfoot. It walks upright and is completely covered in hair. All who have seen this strange creature insist that it is not a chimp or gorilla. It is also not human. It is something in between. Bigfoot is something that science cannot explain.

A hairy giant known as Bigfoot could not possibly be real. Or could it?

CHAPTER 1
Cryptids

There are many things about our world that we understand through scientific study. We know why giraffes have long necks, how gravity works, and what causes earthquakes. But there are other things—unusual, mysterious, and sometimes downright scary—that no one has yet been able to explain. Some of these mysteries have existed for a very long time. For centuries, people from all around the world have reported seeing frightening monsters in remote locations.

The science of studying mysterious, unknown beings is called cryptozoology. "Crypto" means "hidden," and "zoology" means the "study of animals." A cryptid is a creature that may or may not exist. Bigfoot is just one—but perhaps the most famous—example of a cryptid.

Lesser-known cryptids include the Bunyip, an Australian water beast rumored to swallow humans whole, and the Windigo, a scary zombie-like giant who lives in Canada.

Bunyip

Some people feel that cryptozoology is not a real science. Others, however, point to the fact that previously unknown animals are being discovered all the time. Some animals that were thought to be extinct or existed only in legend turned out to be quite real!

The Vikings told tales of a giant sea monster called the Kraken that could wrap its deadly tentacles around a ship and pull it underwater. Few modern people believed that a monster like the Kraken really existed. But in 2004, Japanese researchers photographed images of a previously undiscovered giant squid that was around twenty-six feet long! Another giant squid was later discovered that was fifty-nine feet in length and weighed almost a ton. Even bigger ones might exist in the ocean, as yet undiscovered. Could this be the Kraken?

Then there was the case of the coelacanth (say: SEEL-uh-kanth), a giant fish that could grow more than six feet long and weigh about two hundred pounds. It existed over 360 million years ago and was thought to be extinct. In 1938, however, a live coelacanth was caught off the coast of South Africa. And now we know that there are two rare species of coelacanth living in the world today.

There have been many more previously unknown creatures that were discovered in the wild and later classified by scientists. The list of such animals includes Komodo dragons, giant pandas, and gorillas.

One of the oldest cryptid mysteries is whether there are large, hairy, humanlike beings living deep within wild forests.

The Most Famous Cryptids

Bigfoot is North America's most famous cryptid. But Europe's most famous is the Loch Ness Monster, also known as "Nessie." It is a giant dinosaur-like monster that lives within a lake—a loch—in Scotland. Another well-known cryptid is the Yeti, a furry monster that lives in the Himalayan mountains. The Chupacabra, or goatsucker, is found mostly in Puerto Rico and Central and South America. And the Jersey Devil is a winged beast that lives in the Pine Barrens of southern New Jersey.

Chupacabra

Giant apes once lived on Earth. Scientists know this because in 1935, a German scientist named Gustav Heinrich Ralph von Koenigswald purchased a giant tooth in a Chinese drugstore. That tooth turned out to be a fossil of an extinct creature known as Gigantopithecus. These were massive beasts that lived millions of years ago in East Asia. They stood perhaps over ten feet tall and weighed five hundred pounds or more.

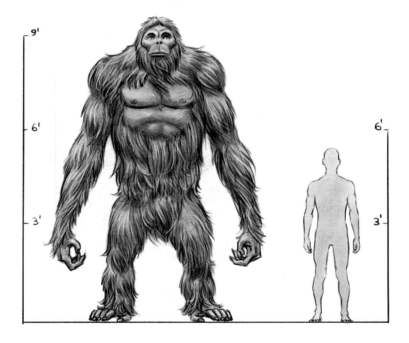

At some point before the Gigantopithecus became extinct, scientists believe that it may have occasionally walked on two legs like humans.

But what if the Gigantopithecus didn't die out? What if a few of them survived by hiding in remote forests or deep caves?

If Bigfoot exists, could it be a descendent of the Gigantopithecus?

CHAPTER 2
Wildmen

The name "Bigfoot" was not introduced until the late 1950s, but for centuries before that there were many stories and sightings of a hairy, often very tall, humanlike beast. They were often described as "wildmen." These creatures tended to live in hidden locations that made it hard for humans to find them. Stories about wildmen had been told for centuries in many countries,

including China, Greece, and England. *The Epic of Gilgamesh*, a story written in Mesopotamia around 2000 BC, tells of a giant wildman called Enkidu who had "hair that sprouted like grain."

Enkidu

Centuries ago, the people in Greece told stories featuring satyrs. These were creatures that looked like humans but also had animal body parts, such as hooves and horns.

Around the year AD 77, a Roman named Pliny the Elder published a book called *Natural*

Satyr

History. In his book, he described many monsters from around the world, including some with dog heads, horse hooves, and long, hairy tails.

Years later, a Greek historian named Arrian wrote a book about the great soldier and ruler Alexander the Great. The book told a tale of Alexander's army battling hairy beasts near the Indus River in Asia. After a bloody fight, some

Alexander the Great

of the mysterious beasts were killed, some escaped into the hills, and some were captured.

Arrian wrote, "Those captured were hairy, not only their heads but the rest of their bodies; their nails were rather like beasts' claws."

The origin and identity of these creatures still remains a mystery.

Then there is the long poem known as *Beowulf*. It was believed to be written over a thousand years ago and is one of the earliest surviving documents written in the English language. It tells the story of an oversize, hairy monster known as Grendel who battles a brave warrior named Beowulf. Grendel has powerful claws and is so strong that he can defeat dozens of men at a time. The story of *Beowulf* is still read and studied today, proving the lasting impression of monsters on our imaginations.

Beowulf and Grendel fight

When European explorers first began exploring the world, they discovered many strange creatures that they had never seen before. One unusual discovery was a hairy manlike animal found in Southeast Asia. The Europeans gave it the name *orangutan*, which means "man of the forest." Today, we know that orangutans are great apes that live in Borneo and Sumatra.

Over the years, as more and more of the world was explored and classified, many people stopped believing in the existence of wildmen. Although our human ancestors were covered with hair, that was millions of years ago. Scientists concluded that the modern world was made up of humans and animals. Anything between those two categories no longer existed.

Or were they just waiting to be discovered?

CHAPTER 3
Wildmen in America

Although scientists decided that giant wildmen did not exist, that didn't stop people from believing in all sorts of creatures. During the nineteenth

century, newspapers in the United States began featuring stories about wildmen living in dark forests at the edges of towns.

In 1811, an explorer who was hiking near the Rocky Mountains in Canada discovered giant track prints belonging to an unknown being. The First Nations people who lived in the area told the explorer that the footprints belonged to

a creature that walked on its two rear legs. They explained that these mysterious beings were large and hairy, and they mostly moved about during the night. They sometimes howled or whistled, and they always smelled very bad.

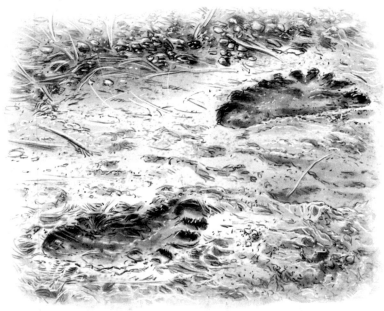

The first newspaper in the United States to publish a story about a wildman sighting was the *Exeter Watchman* in New Hampshire. In the edition dated September 22, 1818,

The writer Mark Twain decided to have some fun with the public's interest in wildmen. In 1869, he wrote a humorous story for the *Buffalo Express* newspaper in New York in which he claimed to have met a wildman.

Mark Twain

"There has been so much talk about the mysterious 'wild man' out there in the West for some time, that I finally felt it was my duty to go out and interview him," wrote Twain. "I felt that the story of his life must be a sad one—a story of suffering, disappointment, and exile."

Twain described the creature "as being hairy, long-armed, and of great strength and stature; ugly and cumbrous; avoiding men, but appearing suddenly and unexpectedly to women and children; going armed with a club, but never molesting any creature, except sheep or other prey; fond of eating and drinking, and not particular about the quality, quantity, or character of the beverages and edibles; living in the woods like a wild beast, but never angry; moaning, and sometimes howling, but never uttering articulate sounds."

Mark Twain's description of a "wild man"

Mark Twain's interview was not meant to be taken seriously, but that didn't stop a lot of people from believing that wildmen really existed. Sightings of wildmen and stories about them continued to appear in books, magazines, and newspapers throughout the following decades. In 1912, the writer Edgar Rice Burroughs created one of the most popular fictional wildmen of all time: Tarzan. The public was fascinated by Burroughs's story of a boy who was raised by apes and later chose to live his life as an ape-man.

Then, in the middle of the twentieth century, the wildman received a new name.

CHAPTER 4
Introducing Bigfoot

Wildmen continued to capture people's imaginations during the twentieth century. In

William Roe

1955, a man named William Roe made an important discovery. It happened when he was hiking in the mountains of British Columbia in Canada. One day, he encountered an amazing sight. It was a giant creature that he described as part animal, part human. It was covered in dark brown fur, and it had long arms that reached down to its knees as it walked upright.

In a sworn statement he later made, Roe said, "It came to the edge of the bush I was hiding in, within twenty feet of me . . . close enough to see that its teeth were white and even. My first impression was that of a huge man, almost six feet tall, almost three feet wide, and probably weighing somewhere near three hundred pounds."

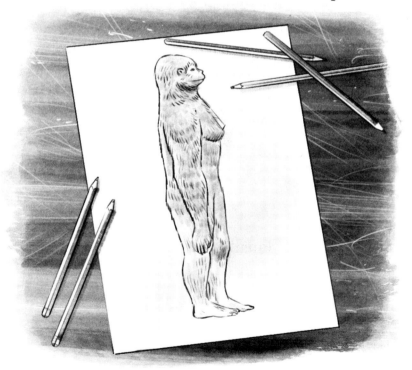

Roe's description of Bigfoot as sketched by his daughter

Roe added, "Finally, the wild thing must have got my scent, for it . . . straightened up to its full height and started to walk rapidly back the way it had come. For a moment it watched me over its shoulder as it went, not exactly afraid but

as though it wanted no contact with anything strange."

Three years after Roe told his story, another event took place that may have revealed the first hard evidence of the creature. In 1958, a man named Jerry Crew was working for a logging company in Northern California. One day, he noticed very large, manlike bare footprints in the ground. Crew made a plaster mold of one of the footprints.

The mysterious footprint was sixteen inches long, which was twice the size of an average human footprint. Soon, the California newspapers featured stories with the word "Bigfoot" in the headlines. The wildman of North America had been renamed.

Were the tracks that Jerry Crew found really from Bigfoot? Not according to one man, Michael Wallace. After his father, Ray Wallace, died in 2002, Michael revealed a pair of large handmade wooden feet and claimed that his father had used them to create the Bigfoot tracks in 1958. But not everyone believed Michael Wallace's story.

In the years after 1958, there were actually *thousands* more Bigfoot sightings in the Pacific Northwest! And many more footprint molds were made to preserve the creature's tracks.

One famous sighting occurred in the city of Fort Bragg along the California coast. A logger named Robert Hatfield was visiting his sister and brother-in-law. On the night of February 7, 1962,

he heard the family's dogs frantically barking in the front yard. Hatfield stepped outside to investigate and was amazed to discover a giant creature. He said the beast was "much bigger than a bear, covered with fur, with a flat, hairless face and perfectly round eyes." He said that it stood "chest and shoulders above a six-foot-high fence."

Hatfield ran into the house and woke Bud Jenkins, his brother-in-law. When the two men returned to the yard, the creature was no longer standing there. Jenkins rushed back inside to grab his gun, and Hatfield ran around the corner of the house, right into the beast! It pushed him down so roughly that his arms and shoulders were "sore for the next three days."

Hatfield rushed back into the house, screaming that there was a "half-man, half-beast" monster outside. He tried to slam the front door shut, but the creature had already grabbed the door and was pushing it in. Jenkins and Hatfield strained against the door. Jenkins held his shotgun, ready to fire at the creature if necessary.

Just as Jenkins was about to fire a shot after telling Hatfield to move away, the beast let go of the door and ran off. That turned out to be a lucky break for the two men, who soon realized that Jenkins's gun wasn't even loaded!

The next day, a sheriff arrived to investigate the incident. There was a foul odor in the air, and the sheriff discovered a large, dirty handprint on the front door of the house. The print was eleven and a half inches long! It had short, thick fingers.

A search party explored the nearby woods, where they found broken branches along a path not far from the Jenkins house. But they did not find the beast.

The newspaper account of the incident was just one of many such Bigfoot stories to appear in print. For the next few years, many nearby newspapers had reported eyewitness accounts of large, half-man, half-beast monsters. The creatures had been spotted in areas ranging from Canada to Northern California.

The North American Bigfoot was quickly becoming one of the most famous cryptids in the world.

CHAPTER 5
Captured on Film!

In October of 1967, Roger Patterson and Bob Gimlin set off on horseback in search of Bigfoot. The two men traveled to the Bluff Creek region

in Northern California, not far from where Jerry Crew had discovered Bigfoot tracks in the ground one decade earlier.

On the afternoon of October 20, Patterson
and Gimlin were riding alongside a creek when
they came to an uprooted tree. Suddenly, both
horses became frightened. As Gimlin later
described it, the animals "started jumping around."

The men looked ahead to see what was scaring the animals.

About one hundred twenty-five yards away—about the length of a soccer field—was an actual Bigfoot, crouching by the edge of the water.

According to an article in the *Los Angeles Times*, this is what the two men saw:

"Its head was very human, though considerably more slanted, with a large forehead and wide, broad nostrils. Its arms hung almost to its knees when it walked. Its hair was two to four inches long, brown underneath, lighter at the top, and covering the entire body except for the face around the nose, mouth, and cheek. And it was female."

Bigfoot as described by Patterson and Gimlin

Patterson's terrified horse reared up, throwing him to the ground. He quickly reached into a bag to grab his movie camera. Gimlin stood by with a gun trained on the Bigfoot,  although he later said he had no intention to shoot the creature unless she became violent.

Patterson turned on the movie camera and started filming the Bigfoot. His short film lasted for only about a minute until the film in his camera ran out. According to Patterson, the

Bigfoot seemed relaxed, as if she "had seen people before."

Patterson's film was not perfect. It was sometimes blurry and shaky. Some parts of the film showed nothing but the ground.

"Roger had the camera up to his eye," Gimlin later recalled. "And he stumbled and fell."

Patterson had started filming the Bigfoot just as she was standing up and walking away. Just before the film ended, she turned her head and looked back over her shoulder at the two men. After that, she disappeared into the woods.

"I thought this was unreal," said Gimlin. "The way it was moving, the mass of muscle."

Patterson and Gimlin were ecstatic—they had evidence that Bigfoot did exist!

Bob Titmus, a man who had studied other Bigfoot tracks, visited the site and made molds of ten footprints. The casts showed that each foot was about fourteen and a half inches long and had five toes, like a human foot. The sole

of each foot was flat. Titmus determined that the footprints appeared to be real and made by a walking creature.

Over the course of the next five decades, many people studied Roger Patterson's film. Researchers and scientists analyzed it frame by frame. Bigfoot fans watched it over and over on the internet. Some declared that the short movie was authentic. Others claimed that it was a fake and showed a person wearing a gorilla suit.

A few people even came forward to claim that they were involved in the hoax, but their stories didn't match up.

A researcher at the Smithsonian Institution called the Patterson film a fraud, as did scientists at the American Museum of Natural History. But in 1994, Russian scientists from the Darwin Museum in Moscow said that the movie could be real. And an American anthropologist named Grover Krantz thought the film was very convincing.

Grover Krantz

"No matter how the Patterson film is analyzed, its legitimacy has been repeatedly supported," said Krantz. "The size and shape [of the Bigfoot] cannot be duplicated by a man, its weight and movements correspond with each other and equally rule out a human subject; its anatomical details are just too good."

Grover Krantz inspects one of the footprint casts

A Bigfoot expert named Loren Coleman reported that the film had been examined by the North American Science Institute—at a cost of over $70,000. The institute declared that the footage was real. According to Coleman, they "suggested that

Loren Coleman

the creature's skin and musculature are what one would expect to find in a living animal, not in a hairy suit, however innovatively it was constructed."

Some researchers have tried filming recreations of the Bigfoot encounter in the same area where Patterson made his film. Others have created computer-animated versions of the incident that can be frozen frame by frame and studied.

And there have been a staggering number of stories written about the event.

Over five decades of arguments and analysis have yet to determine if the movie really does show Bigfoot. However, both Bigfoot believers and nonbelievers agree on one thing: The Patterson film is one of the most important events in Bigfoot history.

CHAPTER 6
Going Global

Since William Roe allegedly spotted a Bigfoot in western Canada in 1955, there have been many more sightings of the creature in the forests of California, Oregon, Washington, and other parts of Canada.

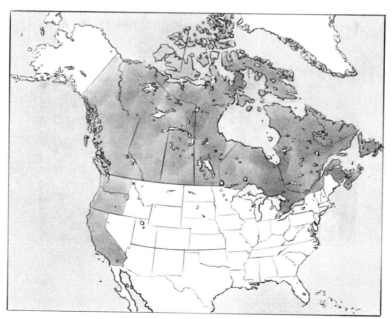

Baby Bigfoot

Roger Patterson's film is not the only one to capture a camera-shy Bigfoot. In 1997, a man named Doug Pridgen shot a short video of a creature that has come to be known as the "New York Baby Bigfoot." The video, shot in the Catskill region of New York State, shows something swinging high in the branches of a tree. It looked to be about two feet long, weighing around twenty pounds.

WITNESS VIDEO

The small apelike creature hops off the shoulder of a larger figure and performs some amazing moves high in the tree branches. Bigfoot researcher Cliff Barackman thinks that the creature could have been a baby Bigfoot, playing in the forest with one of its parents.

Gregg Dancho, director at Connecticut's Beardsley Zoo, studied the film and concluded that the beast is neither bear nor human. "I wouldn't be surprised if something's out there that hasn't been discovered yet. I would not be surprised at all," said Dancho.

According to most people who have seen Bigfoot in various places in North America, it stands somewhere between six and eight feet tall and weighs around eight hundred pounds. It has a thick body, very long arms, and a hunched back. Based on its tracks, the creature's feet are usually about sixteen inches long. Bigfoot also smells really bad, like rotting meat or dead animals.

People who have encountered Bigfoot report that it makes a variety of noises, including howls and raspy screeches. It also sometimes emits a high-pitched whistle. Some think that Bigfoot is imitating other creatures in the forest, including owls and coyotes.

No one knows if there is a Bigfoot language, but a geologist named Alan Berry thinks that Bigfoots may be able to speak to each other. Berry was conducting Bigfoot research in the Sierra mountains in California during the early 1970s,

and one night he heard strange sounds near his campsite. He turned on a tape recorder and captured the noises.

"The sounds carried through the trees as I have never heard human voices carry ever before or since," he said. "And it whistled, a clear beautiful whistle like a bird might make." Berry believed that he was hearing two creatures calling back and forth to each other.

The next morning, Berry discovered several large footprints in the ground nearby and made casts of them.

A professor of electrical engineering at the University of Wyoming listened to the recordings and said the vocal range of the voices was wider than most humans could produce. A navy expert later declared that the voices captured an actual language. Another man actually created a Bigfoot alphabet after he studied the recordings.

In 1989, there were reports that a man named Kenneth Sam had spotted an eight-foot-tall Bigfoot on the Fort Bidwell Paiute Indian reservation in Modoc County, California. The creature was walking on two feet, and when Sam shined a flashlight on it from forty yards away, the Bigfoot first ran toward him but then turned around and fled.

"It was big, dark and hairy looking," Sam told investigators. "It's got silver eyes and it moves pretty fast. . . . It seems like it just glides. I thought  an antelope is fast, but this guy is pretty fast." He added that the beast did not appear to be dangerous, but instead seemed "curious."

Outside of North America, people have also seen mysterious apelike beings that share some of the characteristics of Bigfoot. These creatures have many different names. The Yowie in Australia has been reported to be twelve feet tall. The Orang Pendek (meaning "short person") in Indonesia is shorter than an average person and—unlike Bigfoot—stands only four to five feet tall. In Florida, there is a seven-foot-tall creature called the Skunk

Ape. It gets its name from its terrible smell.

And then there is the Yeti. Its name is an English mispronunciation of the Tibetan "Yeh-Teh," which means "animal of rocky places." The Yeti is sometimes also called Meh-Teh (meaning "man-bear") or the Abominable Snowman. It lives in the Himalayan mountains. But Yeti have sometimes been sighted in the Siberia region of Russia. In movies and books, the Yeti is often shown as having white fur. But those who have seen the Yeti claim that it is covered in black or brown hair. It is over six feet tall and walks upright like a human.

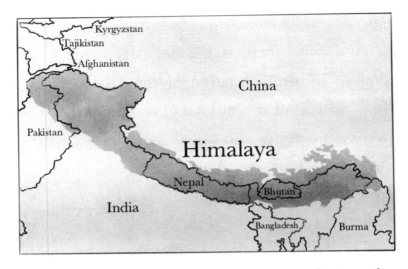

Reports of Yetis began appearing during the 1800s. Europeans who started exploring the Himalayas brought back stories of wildmen in the snowy peaks of the mountains. Native residents in the Himalayas confirmed sightings of what they called furry, upright, tailless demons: Yeh-Teh.

In the 1930s, a team of explorers were climbing Mount Everest, the highest peak of the Himalayas, located at the border of Nepal and Tibet. They discovered large footprints in the snow that measured thirteen inches long. Their local guides told them that the footprints were made by a Yeti.

One of the most famous Yeti attacks took place in 1974. A teenage girl named Lhakpa Dolma was taking care of a herd of yaks high in the Himalayan mountains. One day, a giant beast covered in brown fur came running toward her. It was a Yeti! She tried to run away, but the Yeti grabbed her and tossed her into an icy river. It then killed three of the yaks. By the time Lhakpa emerged from the river, the Yeti was gone. All that remained were the beast's large footprints in the ground.

Bigfoot vs. Yeti

Bigfoot and the Yeti are not the same creature. For one thing, their footprints are quite different. Bigfoot has a more humanlike footprint. The Yeti footprint is closer to a chimpanzee, with one offset toe that resembles a thumb more than it does a big toe. In terms of temper, Bigfoot and Yeti are also quite different. Bigfoot seems more curious than dangerous, and reports of Bigfoot attacks are quite rare. The Yeti has a reputation for violence and has been rumored to attack and kill humans.

Bigfoot

Yeti

In North America, the hunt for a verified Bigfoot sighting continues. Some people have attached video cameras to trees, hoping to record Bigfoot activity during the night. Some have used special devices that can capture the body heat of a Bigfoot even in the darkest forest.

According to a group called the Bigfoot Field Researchers Organization, there have been more than 3,500 Bigfoot sightings and footprint discoveries in North America during the last six decades!

CHAPTER 7
Bigfoot's Big Feet

Bigfoot got its name from its giant feet. And the creature's oversize footprints are important clues when trying to determine if Bigfoot really exists. Scientists believe that studying footprints may be the key to proving that Bigfoot is real.

In the years following the first Bigfoot tracks discovered by Jerry Crew, thousands of footprint tracks, perhaps belonging to Bigfoot, have been studied. A Bigfoot researcher named René Dahinden has found over one thousand giant footprints!

René Dahinden

Most Bigfoot tracks show feet with five long

toes, but there have been other tracks with anywhere from two to six toes. Although the average length of the foot is usually around sixteen inches, some footprints have been found with a length of twenty-seven inches!

A professor at Washington State University analyzed some Bigfoot tracks and estimated that the prints came from a creature weighing five hundred pounds or more. The professor also concluded that the Bigfoot likely had a greatly enlarged ankle bone to support its heavy weight.

Jeff Meldrum is a professor at Idaho State University and an expert on Bigfoot. In a 2020 interview, he said, "I study and teach anatomy, the branch of science that deals with the structure of humans' and animals' bodies. Based on evidence I've seen, I'm convinced that Bigfoot exists. Over the past twenty-four years, I've examined more than three hundred huge footprints that belong to a creature that walks on two legs. They're too big to be human, and they don't match the footprints of any other known animal. Also, mysterious unidentified hair samples have been found near some footprints."

Jeff Meldrum

Thousands of Bigfoot tracks have been observed in the wild, and many of them have been used to make plaster models that are then studied. Close observations reveal that many of the models—called casts—have fingerprint-like ridges or scars that would be difficult to create in a fake footprint.

Do these giant, realistic-looking footprints prove that Bigfoot is real? Until an actual Bigfoot turns up—dead or alive—these footprints might be the best evidence we have of Bigfoot's existence.

The Science of Footprints

Footprints or shoe prints that are created when a person steps into mud, snow, sand, paint, or some other substance are called plastic prints. Crime scene investigators create casts, also known as 3D models, of the prints. They do this by mixing together water and a fine powder to create something called dental stone. They pour the mixture along the inside of the footprints, allowing it to fill the entire area. The dental stone hardens and produces a cast of the footprint. Investigators can then study the

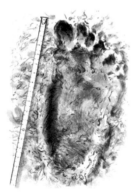

pattern of ridges, curves, and lines made by the bottom of a foot. Footprints can give clues about a person's or animal's movement and can reveal if a person was running, based on the stride of the prints.

CHAPTER 8
Fakes and Frauds

One of the biggest challenges facing Bigfoot researchers is the fact that there have been some known Bigfoot hoaxes over the years. A lot of pranksters have tried to fool the public with fake Bigfoot appearances, remains, or footprints.

One of the most famous hoaxes took place long ago, in 1869. The petrified body of a ten-foot-tall man was discovered in Cardiff, New York. Crowds of people paid fifty cents to view the body. Many claimed that it proved that giant wildmen had once walked on Earth . . . and perhaps still did. Even when the hoax was later revealed to be a statue that had been sculpted by stonecutters, people continued to wonder if wildmen existed.

In 1924, a gold miner named Fred Beck told the Portland *Oregonian* newspaper that giant apes had attacked his camp one night, throwing rocks at his cabin. The next

morning, Beck discovered giant footprints in the ground outside his cabin. The newspaper called it the "Ape Canyon" incident.

It wasn't until sixty years later, in 1982, that a man named Rant Mullens admitted that he was responsible for the Ape Canyon event. He said

Elderly Man Says He Started 'Bigfoot' Legend With Prank

that he had been the one to throw the rocks at Beck's cabin. He also created giant wooden feet that he had pressed into the ground to create the footprints and the hoax. However, not everyone believed Mullens's story.

In the late 1960s, a retired air force pilot named Frank Hansen announced that he had discovered a frozen wildman. He called it the "Minnesota Iceman" and exhibited it for several years at carnivals in the midwestern United States.

It was six feet tall, and its entire body was covered with hair. Cryptid enthusiasts studied the frozen body and declared that it was a previously unknown species. But then a scientist at the Smithsonian Institution examined the body and discovered that it was just another hoax made out of rubber and hair.

In 2008, there was big news that two men had discovered a Bigfoot body in northern Georgia. Matthew Whitton and Rick Dyer reported that they had been on a hike in the woods when they discovered the body of a dead Bigfoot near a stream. The creature looked to be part human

and part ape. It was seven feet, seven inches tall and weighed more than five hundred pounds. Its feet were sixteen and three-quarters inches long. And it smelled very bad.

Whitton and Dyer arranged to have the Bigfoot body frozen. Soon, newspapers, television, and the internet were filled with stories about the amazing discovery. A cryptozoological group called Searching for Bigfoot, Inc. paid $50,000 to obtain the body. The organization held a press conference on August 15, 2008, that was attended by CNN, Fox News, and other national news outlets.

During the press conference, Whitton said, "We were not looking for Bigfoot . . . But you've got to come to terms with it and realize you've got something special. And that's what it was."

The next day, the Searching for Bigfoot group began the process of thawing the creature. As the ice began to melt, they quickly discovered that

Dyer and Whitton speak at the press conference

the body wasn't real. It was just a rubber Bigfoot costume with hair added to it. Whitton and Dyer were forced to admit that it had been a hoax. They had even filled the costume with dead animals and leftover meat, hoping that the bad smell would make it seem more realistic.

CHAPTER 9
Supernatural Sightings

The science of Bigfoot involves studying footprints and analyzing pictures, sounds, videos, and hair samples. There is also a scientific theory that Bigfoot could be a descendent of the extinct

giant ape known as Gigantopithecus. However, there are stories of Bigfoot encounters that science can't explain at all. For example, some people have reported spotting Bigfoot on one side of a riverbank. Seconds later, the creature vanishes and then reappears on the other side of the river. In some cases, a Bigfoot has vanished in a flash of light or slowly turned invisible while being watched by a human.

If Bigfoot is just a giant ape that science has yet to classify, such supernatural powers are very difficult to explain.

In 1976, two researchers named B. Ann Slate and Alan Berry published a book called *Bigfoot*, in which they suggested that the creatures might be alien beings sent to Earth from another planet.

Since then, many people have linked sightings of unidentified flying objects (UFOs) with Bigfoot. In 2010, there was an unexplained flash of bright light in the sky over a forest in western Pennsylvania. Shortly after that, a man reported seeing a strange apelike being in the woods near a white object that looked like a spaceship.

A researcher named Stan Gordon has kept careful records of many such Bigfoot-UFO encounters. According to Gordon, "Reports of such mysterious events, which crossed my desk during 2010, originated from forty-nine counties in Pennsylvania." That means Bigfoot may have been sighted in almost 75 percent of the counties in Pennsylvania!

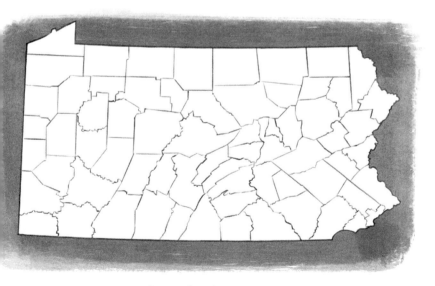

Pennsylvania counties

One of the most famous UFO-related incidents took place in Pennsylvania in 1973. Gordon described what happened:

"Witnesses spotted a slow-moving, bright red UFO apparently land in the pasture of a farm. On the way out to investigate the craft, the group heard a high-pitched whining sound that got louder as they got closer as well as an eerie sound which resembled a baby crying. As they reached the top of the pasture, they were stunned to see the UFO now resembled a white dome which illuminated the entire area. Suddenly, they noticed two Bigfoot creeping along a barbed wire fence about seventy-five feet away from the UFO and making those strange sounds."

What happened next was even more amazing.

"When a witness shot a tracer bullet [a type of bullet that flames brightly when shot] at the creatures, one of the Bigfoot reached up as if to grab it and suddenly, the UFO disappeared into thin air," said Gordon. "The man then tried shooting the Bigfoot with live ammunition, but the bullets had no effect and the creatures wandered off into the woods."

Was the Bigfoot bulletproof or just lucky? No one knows for sure.

Some people who doubt the UFO-Bigfoot connection believe that the reason why no one has ever been able to capture or kill a Bigfoot is because they live "between dimensions," in a world apart from ours, or maybe a completely different reality. According to this theory, Bigfoot is able to disappear and travel to a parallel world that is not defined by our standards of height, width, and depth. Maybe Bigfoot exists in another time and place.

Jack Lapseritis, author of the book *The Psychic Sasquatch and Their UFO Connection*, described this unusual encounter between a group of people and Bigfoot: "After returning from a long hike, the group was stunned when a nine-to-ten-foot Sasquatch stepped out in front of them a short distance away. Then, in the twinkling of an eye, the Bigfoot completely disappeared in front of the witnesses! The witnesses insisted that it literally dematerialized!" It had simply vanished.

Could Bigfoot be an alien visitor from another planet or a supernatural being who lives between dimensions? If so, that could explain why Bigfoot has been so incredibly talented at avoiding humans, not to mention not getting captured or killed by us. Maybe Bigfoot has the ability to appear and disappear from our world in the blink of an eye.

CHAPTER 10
Monster-Mania

So far no one has found a living (or dead) Bigfoot, but that hasn't stopped the creature from showing up in just about every form of popular culture. There are Bigfoot movies, TV shows, songs, and plenty of Bigfoot-themed products.

The 1987 movie *Harry and the Hendersons*

is perhaps the most famous Bigfoot movie. In it, Bigfoot was a lovable, misunderstood creature that moved into the home of the Henderson family after they accidentally hit him with their car while driving through the woods. Actor Peter Hall, who was over seven feet tall, played Bigfoot. The movie was so popular that a TV series based on it aired from 1991 to 1993.

One of the most widely read Bigfoot titles is John Green's 1978 book *Sasquatch: The Apes Among Us*. The book, which documents more than four thousand Bigfoot sightings, was called the "best written book on the subject" by the Bigfoot Field Researchers Organization.

John Green

Green's interest in Bigfoot went back to 1957, when he began investigating sightings and tracks. In 1958, Green traveled to Bluff Creek, California, to examine the tracks that had been discovered by Jerry Crew.

One of the first Bigfoot movie documentaries (a movie that provides factual reporting) was the 1973 film *Sasquatch Among Us*. It has been followed by many more documentary movies, including *Not Your Typical Bigfoot Movie* and *Sasquatch Odyssey: The Hunt for Bigfoot*.

Animal Planet's *Finding Bigfoot* was one of the most popular Bigfoot-themed television series. It premiered in 2011 and ran for seven years. The Travel Channel produced a series called *Expedition Bigfoot*.

Bigfoot images can be seen on everything from baseball caps to lunch boxes, and in television commercials. In 1993, Pizza Hut offered a two-foot-long Bigfoot pizza. But perhaps the most well-known Bigfoot is the one who appears in Jack Link's beef jerky commercials. The company's motto is "Feed your wild side," and they've featured a Sasquatch in over a dozen ads since 2006.

In the northern California town of Willow Creek, near where Jerry Crew discovered giant footprints in the ground in 1958, there is a yearly celebration called Bigfoot Daze. The weekend festival is very popular and features lots of Bigfoot-inspired food, musical performances, and souvenirs. Tourists who visit the fair are warned not to go wandering into the nearby woods!

Was Bigfoot the Inspiration for Chewbacca?

Nope!

They are both shaggy giants that walk upright, but the Star Wars character Chewbacca is definitely *not* a Bigfoot.

Chewbacca is a Wookiee who comes from the planet Kashyyyk, which is located far away in another galaxy. Star Wars creator George Lucas confirmed that he was not thinking of Bigfoot when he created the fuzzy warrior who copilots the *Millennium Falcon.* Lucas has said that his dog Indiana was the inspiration for Chewbacca.

CHAPTER 11
Is Bigfoot Real?

Although there are thousands of eyewitness accounts of people claiming to have seen Bigfoot, no actual creature has ever been captured. Despite the lack of physical proof, there is no shortage of people who believe that Bigfoot exists.

The Bigfoot Field Researchers Organization estimates that there are perhaps two thousand to six thousand Bigfoots living in North America. Most of the Bigfoots are thought to be hiding in remote forests that are very difficult to explore.

Since the early 1960s, there have been roughly 3,500 documented Bigfoot sightings and track finds. The Bigfoot Field Researchers Organization says, "The documented sightings and track finds are thought to represent only a fraction of the actual observations by humans in North America during the same time frame. The reports come from basically everywhere across the continent where there are coniferous forests. It is likely that many observations and track finds over the years involved the same [Bigfoots]. But it is also likely that many Bigfoots have never been observed by any humans."

There are also many nonbelievers, who sometimes wonder why no skeletons of the creature have been found. The Bigfoot Field Researchers Organization has an answer for that: "It is quite possible they bury their dead. . . . This type of behavior demonstrates a form of higher intelligence, so it would make sense that Sasquatch learned to bury their dead to hide the remains."

Some ask why humans have never discovered the home of a Bigfoot. One theory is that Bigfoot might live underground, deep within caves, which are often difficult for people to explore.

As for why a relatively small number of people have actually seen Bigfoot in the wild, some researchers have suggested that the creature may have heightened senses and can tell when people are approaching—maybe by smelling them. That would give Bigfoot plenty of time to hide from humans.

One of the most successful ways to prove the existence of Bigfoot would be to collect DNA samples from the creature. DNA is found in the cells of every living thing. It is the molecule inside of cells that carries instructions for the development and function of all known organisms. DNA determines how everything grows—from onions and oak trees to butterflies and humans . . . and perhaps Bigfoot as well. People leave behind DNA all the time without even thinking about it. Every day, the average person sheds forty to one hundred strands of hair that are full of DNA.

Bigfoot is a very hairy being. Assuming that it sheds, there is the possibility that its hair could be collected—perhaps from trees or bushes—and later analyzed by scientists. Bigfoot researcher James "Bobo" Fay, who has appeared on the *Finding Bigfoot* TV series, says that utility poles

are also a good place to collect evidence because animals use them as scratching posts.

One of the most interesting searches for genuine Bigfoot hair took place in 2012. Veterinarian Melba S. Ketchum studied the DNA of more than one hundred hair samples. She and her researchers concluded that the samples may have come from a creature that somehow developed around 15,000 years ago as a result of a cross between humans and unknown primates. They may have come from Bigfoot.

There have been other studies of possible Bigfoot hair samples, revealing DNA that could not be matched to any known animal.

If scientists are ever able to analyze Bigfoot's DNA, we will finally be able to determine if the creature is more human than ape. Or even if Bigfoot is a part of our world.

The people who believe in Bigfoot point to all the physical evidence that has been collected over the years: photos, videos, and audio recordings. Hair samples and thousands of footprints have also been analyzed.

The main argument against Bigfoot's existence is that no actual Bigfoot—dead or alive—has ever been found.

Still, the search for Bigfoot continues. In 2021, the Bigfoot Field Researchers Organization sponsored more than a dozen North American expeditions to find this mysterious cryptid. The searches ranged from Washington State to Massachusetts.

Over the years, Stan Gordon has continued to gather eyewitness reports of Bigfoot and UFOs. During 2021, three possible Bigfoot incidents took place in different locations around the Chestnut Ridge area in Pennsylvania.

"In late January, a resident reported loud howls and vocalizations unlike that of any native animal such as coyotes that the witness was familiar with," said Gordon. "In February, a witness reported observing a 7–8 feet tall hair covered creature in daylight. Later that month, a series of 5-toed footprints with a large stride between them were observed in the snow."

The quest to discover if Bigfoot is real leads

to a place where legend and science meet. Many people claim to have seen Bigfoot. Researchers have tried to confirm these sightings—so far without success. Does that mean that Bigfoot does not exist?

Because some fantastic creatures that no one believed in have turned out to actually exist, maybe Bigfoot does, too.

But Bigfoot is still *real*.

Bigfoot lives in our imaginations. He is part of American folklore, and stories about him have been passed from one generation to the next.

He is exciting and interesting because we continue to search for answers, and we want to learn the truth. He is the most popular cryptid for a reason: Even if we've never met Bigfoot, we'll recognize him instantly when we do.

Timeline of Bigfoot

1811 — An explorer discovers giant track prints belonging to an unknown creature in the Canadian Rocky Mountains

1818 — The first American newspaper story about a wildman sighting is published in the *Exeter Watchman*

1924 — A miner named Fred Beck claims that apelike creatures attacked his camp

1935 — Ralph von Koenigswald discovers a Gigantopithecus fossil in China

1955 — William Roe encounters a Bigfoot in the mountains of British Columbia in Canada

1958 — Jerry Crew discovers Bigfoot tracks near his campsite

— The name "Bigfoot" appears in print for the first time

1967 — Roger Patterson films a Bigfoot in California

1976 — In their book *Bigfoot*, B. Ann Slate and Alan Berry suggest Bigfoot might be an alien being from another world

2012 — Veterinarian Melba S. Ketchum conducts a study of potential Bigfoot DNA samples

2021 — Three possible Bigfoot incidents are reported in Pennsylvania

— The Bigfoot Field Researchers Organization sponsors over a dozen expeditions in North America

Timeline of the World

1809 — Abraham Lincoln is born

1818 — Mary Shelley's *Frankenstein; or, the Modern Prometheus* is published

1861 — The US Civil War begins

1896 — The first modern Olympic Games take place in Greece

1903 — The Wright brothers make the first controlled flight in an airplane

1914 — The Panama Canal opens

1927 — Charles Lindbergh makes the first solo flight over the Atlantic Ocean

1939 — Batman makes his debut in *Detective Comics* #27

1945 — The United Nations is founded

1954 — The first Godzilla movie is released in Japan

1963 — US president John F. Kennedy is assassinated

1969 — Astronaut Neil Armstrong is the first person to walk on the moon

1987 — The world population reaches five billion

1994 — Disney's *The Lion King* movie is released

2008 — Barack Obama is elected as the first African American president of the United States

2015 — Liquid water is found on Mars

Bibliography

*Books for young readers

*Brockenbrough, Martha. *Finding Bigfoot: Everything You Need to Know*. New York: Feiwel and Friends, 2013.

Buhs, Joshua Blu. *Bigfoot: The Life and Times of a Legend*. Chicago: The University of Chicago Press, 2009.

Burnette, Tom, and Rob Riggs. *Bigfoot: Exploring the Myth & Discovering the Truth*. Woodbury: Llewellyn Publications, 2014.

Bynum, Joyce. "Bigfoot—A Contemporary Belief Legend." *ETC: A Review of General Semantics*, Vol. 49, no. 3 (Fall 1992). New York: Institute of General Semantics.

*Claybourne, Anna. *Don't Read This Book Before Bed: Thrills, Chills, and Hauntingly True Stories*. Washington, DC: National Geographic Partners, 2017.

Loxton, Daniel, and Donald R. Prothero. *Abominable Science!: Origins of the Yeti, Nessie, and Other Famous Cryptids*. New York: Columbia University Press, 2013.

Meldrum, Jeff. "Is Bigfoot Real?" **Scholastic News**, January 27, 2020. Jefferson City: Scholastic Inc.

*Peabody, Erin, and Victor Rivas. **Bigfoot (Behind the Legend)**. New York: Little Bee Books, 2017.

Redfern, Nick. **The Bigfoot Book: the Encyclopedia of Sasquatch, Yeti, and Cryptid Primates**. Canton: Visible Ink Press, 2015.

*Townsend, John. **Bigfoot and Other Mysterious Creatures**. New York: Crabtree Publishing, 2008.

*Worth, Bonnie. **Looking for Bigfoot**. Step into Reading. New York: Penguin Random House, 2010.

*Yorke, Malcolm. **Beastly Tales**. New York: DK Publishing, 1998.

YOUR HEADQUARTERS FOR HISTORY

Activities, Mad Libs, and sidesplitting jokes.
Discover the Who HQ books beyond the biographies